M000228288

JAPANESE

JAPANESE

CREATED BY SETH GODIN
PRODUCED BY CADER BOOKS

Andrews and McMeel
A Universal Press Syndicate Company
Kansas City • New York

ISBN: 0-8362-2630-5

Library of Congress Catalog Card Number: 90-85469

Attention: Schools and Businesses
Andrews and McMeel books are available at quantity discounts with bulk purchase for educational, business, or sales promotional use. For information, please write to: Special Sales Department, Andrews and McMeel, 4900 Main Street, Kansas City, Missouri 64112.

Acknowledgments

The creators gratefully wish to acknowledge the kind and expert assistance of the many people who made this book possible. Translation expertise was provided by Japanese Printing Services and by Hisako Fujii of the Columbia University Student Tutoring and Translation Agency. Thanks are also due to Kathleen O'Connor, Renee Schwartz, and David Sultanik for their support roles.

Everyone at Andrews and McMeel has been enthusiastic and supportive from the initiation of this project. We are particularly grateful for the sharp editorial eye of Donna Martin and the friendship and support of Tom Thornton and Kathleen Andrews.

How to Use This Book

This book is specially designed to be the only phrasebook that you can use successfully even if you have no knowledge at all of the foreign language. Each of the standard pages in the book contains one phrase in large type, with the English version below it. If you can turn a page, you can use this book to be understood in Japanese.

To find the phrase you want, flip through the book using the index triangles at the top corner of each page (Customs, Police, Lodging, Reference, Dining, Shopping, Transport) and the key-word phrase summaries along the bottom of each page.

Fold back the book so the phrase you want is on top and then hold the book up like a flashcard to a native so that they can see it. They'll be able to read the large print translation without confusion and help you on your way.

Certain pages require that you make a choice, between mineral water with or without bubbles, for example. Either circle your preference, or indicate it with your finger when holding up the book.

The "Directions" section combines three different

destinations on each page. Just use your finger to point to the destination you need or circle it with a pencil.

There are special pages covering common drugstore items (found in Shopping), conditions requiring medical assistance (found at the back of the book), and allergies or substances to which you are very sensitive (also found at the back of the book). For these sections, use a pencil to circle the appropriate phrase or phrases before you show it to someone. The Menu Decoder will help you figure out some common menu items.

Throughout the book, we have intentionally not taken the exhaustive approach used by other phrasebooks. This book contains 100 key questions and phrases and numerous special features, all designed to address essential needs while traveling—when you get in trouble, are lost, hungry, in need of help, or just plain frustrated by your inability to communicate with other people, this book is a safe and easy way of knowing with certainty that your message will be seen if not heard.

Most of all, don't forget to say *please* and *thank you*, which you'll find at the end of the book. You'll be amazed at what a difference it makes. We hope this book shows you the way to happier trip.

どこで見つけられますか:

Where can I find:

☐ 良いレストラン

A good restaurant

☐ 良いショッピングの場所

Good shopping

☐ 海岸（ビーチ）

The beach

FOOD/SHOP/SUN

どこで見つけられますか:

Where can I find:

☐ 西洋料理のレストラン

Western restaurants

☐ 日本庭園

Japanese gardens

☐ 寺　院

Temples

LOCAL SIGHTS

どこで見つけられますか:

Where can I find:

☐ ツーリスト・インフォメーション

Tourist information

☐ アメリカン・エクスプレスの事務

American Express office

☐ 両替所施設

Money changing facility

MONEY

どこで見つけられますか:

Where can I find:

☐ アメリカ大使館

The U.S. embassy

☐ 病　院

Medical help

☐ 警　察

The police

HELP

どこで見つけられますか：

Where can I find:

☐ 国際電話のかけられる場所

Overseas telephone

☐ 郵便局

Post Office

☐ 銀　行

Bank

ERRANDS

どこで見つけられますか:

Where can I find:

☐ 入 口

Entrance

☐ 出 口

Exit

☐ 門（ゲート）

The gate

IN/OUT

どこで見つけられますか：

Where can I find:

☐ 空　港

Airport

☐ 汽車の駅

Train station

☐ バスの停留所

Bus station

TRANSPORT

どこで見つけられますか：

Where can I find:

□ 地下鉄

The subway

□ タクシー

Taxi

□ 私の滞在しているホテル

My hotel

TRANSPORT

どこで見つけられますか:

Where can I find:

☐ 薬 局

A pharmacy

☐ スーパーマーケット

A supermarket

☐ _____

(write in your own destination)

STORES

お手洗いは どこでしょう？

How do I get to the bathroom?

BATHROOM

私は学生として
ここに
来ています。

I am here as a student.

STUDENT

私はビジネスで
ここに
来ています。

I am here on business.

BUSINESS

私は休暇で
ここに
来ています。

I am here on vacation.

VACATION

申告するものは
何もありません。

I have nothing to declare.

NOTHING

それは個人的に
使用するための
ものです。

It's for personal use.

PERSONAL

それらはここで
買ったものでは
ありません。

I didn't buy those here.

DIDN'T BUY

消費税の払戻しはどうすれば受けられますか？

How do I get a sales tax refund?

TAX REFUND

パスポートを
失くしました。
私はアメリカ
市民です。

I've lost my passport. I'm a citizen of the
United States.

LOST PASSPORT

構わないで下さい、
でなければ
警察を呼びます。

Leave me alone or I will call the police.

STOP

POLICE

すぐに警察を
呼んで下さい。

Call the police immediately!

POLICE

強盗に
あいました。

I've been mugged.

MUGGED

POLICE

私のホテルの
部屋が盗難に
あいました。

My hotel room has been robbed.

ROBBED

この人で
困っています。

This man is bothering me.

BOTHER

犬に
噛まれました。

I was bitten by a dog.

DOG BITE

予約を
してあります。

I have a reservation.

RESERVATION

お湯の出る洗面
所付きの部屋に
して下さい。

I would like a room with hot water.

NO BATH

お手洗いと
浴室付の部屋に
して下さい。

I would like a room with a bathroom.

WITH BATHROOM

二つベッドが
ある部屋に
して下さい。

We want a room with two beds.

TWO BEDS

先に部屋を
見せてもらえ
ますか？

May I look at the room first?

LOOK

お手洗い、
浴室はどこ
でしょう？

Where is the bathroom?

BATHROOM

料金に朝食が含まれていますか?

Is breakfast included?

BREAKFAST

朝食をとらないと、宿泊費は安くなりますか？

Is the room less without breakfast?

WITHOUT BREAKFAST

朝食は何時でしょうか？

What time is breakfast?

BREAKFAST TIME

空室があるか他のホテルに電話して頂けますか？

Could you call another hotel to see if they have a room?

CALL ELSEWHERE

＿泊間滞在
します。

I am staying ___ nights.

LENGTH

ロビーは何時に 閉りますか?

What time does the lobby close?

CLOSING TIME

電話で起こして頂けますか？

Can I have a wake-up call?

WAKE-UP

アメリカに電話を
したい のですが。

I'd like to place a call to the United States.

PHONE CALL

国際電話の
追加料金は
いくらですか？

How much is the international phone
surcharge?

SURCHARGE

部屋に虫が
いるのですが。

There are bugs in my room.

BUGS

余分なタオルを
下さい。

I need extra towels.

TOWELS

クリーニングの
サービスが
ありますか。

Can you have my clothes cleaned?

CLEANING

明日チェックアウトします。

I will check out tomorrow.

CHECK OUT

チェックアウトは何時迄ですか？

What is check out time?

CHECK OUT

ファックスが あれば使わせて 頂けますか？

Do you have a fax that I may use?

FAX

英語の話せる
ガイドが
必要です。

I need a guide who speaks English.

GUIDE

通訳が必要です。

I need a translator.

TRANSLATOR

誰か英語の
話せる人の所に
連れて行って
下さい。

Please take me to someone who speaks
English.

TRANSLATION

おいくらですか？

How much will it cost?

COST

米国へこれを送るのにいくらかかりますか?

How much to send this to the United States?

SHIP

トラベラーズ チェックで かまいませんか?

Do you take travelers checks?

TRAVELERS CHECKS

クレジット カードが 使用できますか？

Do you take charge cards?

CREDIT CARDS

それを書いて頂けますか？

Would you write that down?

IN WRITING

領収書を下さい。

Give me a receipt please.

RECEIPT

地図を
頂けますか。

I'd like a map.

MAP

ここから
歩くには
遠すぎますか？

Is it too far to walk there?

TOO FAR

どのくらい かかりますか？

How long will it take?

HOW LONG

そこは町の安全な地域ですか？

Is it in a good area of town?

SAFE

雨が降る でしょうか？

Is it supposed to rain?

RAIN

営業時間は
何時から何時迄
でしょうか？

What are their hours?

HOURS

チップはどのくらいが適当でしょうか？

What tip is appropriate?

TIP

現金料替率は
いくらですか？

What's the exchange rate?

EXCHANGE RATE

私達の
写真を撮って
頂けますか？

Would you take our picture please?

PICTURE

写真を撮っても よろしいですか？

May I take a picture?

PICTURE

残りの席の内で
□ 一番良い席
□ 一番安い席

The best seat/cheapest seat you have left.

SEATING

地元の音楽は
どこで
聴けますか？

Where can we hear local music?

LOCAL MUSIC

学生割り引きが
ありますか？

Do you give a student discount?

STUDENT DISCOUNT

この近くに ユースホステル がありますか？

Is there a youth hostel nearby?

HOSTEL

年配者用の割り引きがありますか？

Is there a Senior Citizen discount?

SENIOR DISCOUNT

身体障害者用の特別な設備がありますか？

Are there special facilities for the handicapped?

HANDICAPPED

どこか値段の手ごろなレストランを教えて頂けますか？

Can you recommend an inexpensive restaurant?

CHEAP

予約してありま
せんが、席が
ありますか？

We don't have reservations. Can you seat us?

NO RESERVATIONS

DINING

どのくらい 待つでしょうか？

How long a wait will it be?

WAIT

静かでロマンティックな席はありますか？

Do you have a quiet, romantic table?

ROMANTIC

この土地特有の
料理が食べたい
のですが。

We want to eat your regional specialty.

SPECIALTY

お薦め品は
何でしょう？

What do you recommend?

牛、豚、鶏肉を
使っていない
料理を
教えて下さい。

Can you recommend something that doesn't
have any beef, pork or chicken?

VEGETARIAN

塩を使っていない
料理を
教えて下さい。

Can you recommend something that doesn't
have any salt?

NO SALT

コレステロールの低い料理を教えて下さい。

Can you recommend something that is low in cholesterol?

NO CHOLESTEROL

低脂肪の料理を
教えて下さい。

Can you recommend something that isn't very
fatty?

LOW FAT

ワインリストを見せて頂けますか？

May we see the wine list?

お水を頂けますか？

May we have some water?

WATER

ボトル入りの
水を下さい。
□ 炭酸入り
□ 炭酸無し

May I have bottled water please? (with bubbles/without bubbles)

BOTTLED WATER

パンをもう少し頂けますか？

May we have some more bread?

BREAD

お勘定を
お願いします。

May we have the check?

CHECK

チップは含まれていますか？

Is the tip included?

Beef 牛 肉	**Mackerel** 鯖
Blowfish ふ ぐ	**Octopus** たこ
Chicken 鶏 肉	**Quail Egg** うずらの卵
Clam はまぐり	**Rice** ご 飯
Crab か に	**Rolled Sushi** 巻寿司
Cuttlefish い か	**Sake (cold)** 酒（冷）
Egg 卵	**Sake (hot)** 酒（燗）
Eggplant なすび	**Salmon** 鮭
Ginger しょうが	**Salmon Roe** いくら
Kobe Steak 神戸ステーキ	**Sashimi** 刺し身

Sea Urchin
　う　に
Shabu Shabu
　しゃぶしゃぶ
Shrimp
　海　老
Soy Sauce
　醤　油
Sushi
　寿　司
Tempura
　天ぷら
Teriyaki
　照り焼き
Tofu
　豆　腐
Tuna
　まぐろ
Vegetables
　野　菜

Wasabi
　わさび
Yakitori
　焼きとり
Yellowtail
　はまち
Japanese Beer
　日本のビール
Green Tea
　緑　茶
Western Food
　西洋料理
Rare
　レアー
Medium
　ミディアム
Well Done
　ウエルダン

ちょっと見せて
もらって
いるだけです。

Thank you, we're just looking

JUST LOOKING

何かバーゲン
セールのものは
ありますか？

Is anything on sale?

SALE

私のサイズはどれくらいだと思いますか？

What size do you think I take?

SIZE

私のアメリカの
サイズは
＿＿＿です。

＿＿＿＿＿＿＿＿＿＿

My American size is

SIZE

もう少し小さい
サイズのが
ありますか？

Do you have a smaller size?

SMALLER

もう少し大きい
サイズのが
ありますか？

Do you have a larger size?

LARGER

サイズの修正をして頂けますか？

Do you do alterations?

ALTERATIONS

値段は安く
なりますか？

Can we bargain on the price?

消費税控除用の
用紙が
ありますか？

Do you have the forms for sales tax
deduction?

TAX FORMS

これは返品
できますか？

Is this returnable?

これを取り替え
たいのですが。

_____

I want to exchange this.

EXCHANGE

色違いのものが
ありますか？

Do you have it in any other colors?

COLORS

絵葉書は
ありますか？

Do you have any postcards?

POSTCARDS

フィルムを
下さい。

I would like some film.

FILM

どこで
手に入りますか:

Where can I find:

Acetamino-phen	非アスピリン系解熱鎮痛剤	Contact lens solution	コンタクトレンズの洗浄液
Allergy pills	アレルギーの薬	Cough syrup	咳止め用シロップ
Antibiotic ointment	抗生物質の塗薬	Cramps medicine	激しい腹痛用の薬（けいれん、生理痛等）
Aspirin	アスピリン	Decon-gestant	鼻詰まりを除く薬
Bandage strips	バンドエイド	Diarrhea medicine	下痢止めの薬
Bug repellent	防虫薬	Sunburn ointment	日焼けの痛み止めの塗薬
Cold remedies	風邪薬	Suntan lotion	日焼け用のローション
Condoms	コンドーム	Tampons	タンポン
Constipation medicine	便秘の薬	Tissues	ティッシュー

この処方箋の
薬を追加して
下さい。

I need this prescription refilled.

PRESCRIPTION

時刻表は
どこですか？

Where is the schedule?

SCHEDULE

☐ 急行列車
☐ 普通列車
にして下さい。

I'd like the express/local train.

TRAIN

☐ 一等席
☐ 二等席
の切符を下さい。

I'd like a first-class/second-class ticket.

TICKET

どのホームから出発しますか？

Which platform does it leave from?

PLATFORM

ドライブして
観光地を
見せて下さい。

Please drive around and show us some of the sights.

SIGHTS

車に酔い易いので
ゆっくり
運転して下さい。

Please go slowly—I get carsick easily.

SLOWER

急いでいますので
速く行って下さい。

Please go quickly—I'm in a hurry.

FASTER

ここから
いくつ目の
駅ですか？

How many stops is it from here?

STOPS

私のフライトの
再確認を
して下さい。

Please reconfirm my flight.

RECONFIRM

お願いします。

_____

Please

PLEASE

ありがとう。

_____

Thank you

THANK YOU

注意： 私の体質に合いません。

Caution: this will make me very sick:

Alcohol	アルコール類	Corn	とうもろこし
Apple	りんご	Dogs	犬
Banana	バナナ	Eggs	卵
Bee stings	ハチ刺され	Fish	魚
Caffeine	カフェイン	Grapefruit	グレープフルーツ
Cats	ねこ	Lettuce	レタス
Cheese	チーズ	Local anesthetic	局部麻酔
Chocolate	チョコレート	MSG	グルタミン酸ソーダ （化学調味料）
Coriander	コエンドロ	Milk	牛乳

注意： 私の体質に合いません。

Caution: this will make me very sick:

Mushroom	きのこ類	Spicy foods	スパイスのきいた辛い料理
Nuts	ナッツ類	Strawberries	いちご
Orange	オレンジ	Sugar	砂　糖
Peanuts	ピーナッツ	Tap water	水道の水
Penicillin	ペニシリン	Tomato	トマト
Sesame seeds	ごまの実	Tropical fruits	トロピカルフルーツ
Shellfish	貝、甲殻類	Wheat	小　麦
Shrimp	海　老	White potato	白いじゃがいも
Soy bean	大　豆	Yeast	イースト菌

体調が
優れません。

I have a medical problem.

Allergies (to food)	アレルギー（食べ物による）	Something in my eye	目に異物が入った
Allergies (hay fever)	アレルギー（花紛症による）	Female trouble	婦人系の異常
Need antibiotic	抗生物質が必要	Feverish	熱 病
Back pain	背中の痛み	Headache	頭 痛
Blood in stool	血 便	Heat exhaustion	日射病
Breathing trouble	呼吸困難	Pain in the prostate	前立腺の痛み
Chest pain	胸の痛み	Sunburn	日焼け
Consti-pation	便 秘	Stomach pain	腹 痛
Diarrhea	下 痢	Throwing up	嘔 吐
Earache	耳の痛み	Tooth	歯